my dearest
BRIDESMAID

my dearest
BRIDESMAID

A HEARTFELT KEEPSAKE
FROM THE BRIDE IN YOUR LIFE

MELANIE J. PELLOWSKI

Skyhorse Publishing

Visit our website at www.skyhorsepublishing.com.

10 9 8 7 6 5 4 3 2 1

Library of Congress Cataloging-in-Publication Data is available on file.

Cover design by Jenny Zemanek
Cover illustration by iStock photo

Print ISBN: 978-1-5107-2684-0
Ebook ISBN: 978-1-5107-2685-7

Printed in China

To the Pellowski and LaPlaca families for helping me down the aisle.
To my parents especially, for guiding me long before that and ever after, and to Nick,
for making a fairy tale wedding the introduction to the rest of our love story as husband and wife.

Table of Contents

Introduction

Something old,
Something new,
Something borrowed,
Something blue,
And a silver sixpence in her shoe

This old English rhyme with curious origins is still respected today as most brides abide by the well-known tradition with a smile and a certainty. After all, the items listed in this classic wedding saying are the go-to good luck itinerary for the bride on her big day. It's kind of a slogan and definitely a superstition. Once a bride tackles each piece of the poem and sets out on her wedding day with bridesmaid bodyguards and some bubbly to boot, her heart will be full of gratitude. Let this book guide you through these next few months and remind you in the years to come—you are appreciated, bridesmaid. You are loved and saluted for all you have done to earn this role. Your loyalty and friendship has been a priceless gift, and your involvement now is even more proof of your status as the ultimate friend.

A BRIDE'S DREAM TEAM

This isn't some lame group of childhood rejects thrown together with little thought. You and the other bridesmaids are the bride's dream team, and you each have an important role to play on the field. Bridesmaids serve as great reminders of what's truly important. The history that true friends share should offer evidence (hopefully not in online photos) that it's okay if everything doesn't always go as planned. Every time you feel frustrated or misunderstood, try to keep in mind why you even decided to sign up for this nonsense. Maybe there are some rules to manning this bridesmaid ship, but aren't the best memories made when friends find innocent ways to stretch the rule book? Keep this process fun and keep it right for you and the bride. So long as the bride has the best of intentions, she should  follow her heart. After all, that's what got her here. You should know, bridesmaid, that's what got you here, too. Let the unique past you share with the bride be your compass to navigating your every move going forward.

My Dearest Bridesmaid

You are my truest friend, most loyal sister, and perhaps even oldest partner in crime. Not old in age, but in wisdom and connection, in the most vibrant way possible. You know me. You speak only of my proudest moments while harboring my most embarrassing times. That's why I hold our friendship dear, after countless good times and bad ones that became better because you were there. Remember that one awful time I did that one terrible thing and wanted to leave the country for fear of embarrassment? You know the one I mean. You would have taken a spontaneous road trip with me, across the bottom of the ocean, if you thought it would have brightened my spirits.

SPIRITS

We drank them instead. Thanks for only speaking of that memory out loud to share a laugh with me, once I was ready to finally laugh about it. Thanks for also never sharing those questionable actions with my future husband. You make my good side shine, a testament of a true girlfriend.

GIRL POWER

Let's celebrate it together, again, because I'm a lucky girl that's finally on her way down the aisle. Not the candy aisle, or the ice cream aisle, or the liquor aisle as per usual. I'm talking about a most important path that leads to a happy ending, and I need you there. You should know why, but if you don't, let these words of our friendship serve as a reminder. After all, our times together have been all sorts of happy, sad, funny, sometimes dangerous and stupid but always entertaining and memorable. Maybe some of those times left us grounded as kids. Now, I need you to keep me grounded as I suit up in a dress we have all dreamt about wearing. This also means laughing with me when I inevitably drip red wine down the front of the pristine thing once my big day is finally here. Sprinkle some club soda on it, like our mothers would always say, always with a sparkle in their smiles.

SPARKLE

As women, we have all worn sparkly tiaras at one point or another in our single lives. We all hold countless sweet sixteen memories as proof. Now, I have an ever important, everlasting sparkle on the band of a special finger. I don't mean the middle one that gets me into trouble when I'm angry.

I mean the one next to that one. It's the one with a promise banded by love. Once a lonely ring finger, it's now covered with a symbol of perpetual love and happiness. That gem is a precious accent of protection. It is the armor we once lied about having so that unwanted creeps would leave us alone. It's a little light that says, "This little girl's heart is taken. She has found her prince." Which, in token, has left me with a royal feeling of wanting to share my love with my court. And so, I have knighted you with a task granted to only the noblest of the noble in my own crazy little world, you know, the one where I will have enough money to one day afford a castle with a moat.

CRAZY

We have taken that adjective by storm in the past, have we not? Knowing everything you have done for me, and everything we have been through together, I am delighted, though not surprised of course, that you have agreed to enlist yourself to stand beside me on my latest journey. You are a warrior, but a fashionable one, except for that one outfit you wore to that one party. I still have that picture in a box for safekeeping, don't you worry. After everything else I have asked you to help me with before, I'm not worried this time. This next adventure should be a piece of cake.

CAKE

How delicious. Thanks, by the way. Thank you for all of those times you reminded me I shouldn't dig into a giant pie at three in the morning after a party. Thank you for the other times you dug in with me when I was digging myself a hole of depression. We've pigged out, vegged out, and partied our brains out. That's exactly the kind of joy I am looking for at my wedding. Honestly, what is a wedding day without a friend like you? Sounds like a party I don't want to attend. It's not only because I need a friend that knows my limits better than I do (especially when champagne is involved). It's not just because I need to know you approve of every big step in my life. It's because you have always been there, through the questionable haircuts and the even more frowned upon (but very fun) class cuts. You are my soul sister. That's an important piece to the puzzle of a girl like me marrying her soul mate on a very special day.

SOUL SISTER

I said yes, a most important decision, and you know that I hardly make decisions without calling you to dissect them first. You are my lifeline to call when I need to phone a friend. Your number is one of the only ones I actually know by heart. You lift my soul to a better place, and your presence and approval confirms I am about to marry a man that makes me want to be a better woman. He makes me want to be a better friend to you. When I walk the walk to say, "I do," I'll feel strong knowing that you said yes, too. Thank you, my dearest bridesmaid, for proving I am a lucky girl whose life is filled with all sorts of precious love.

Something Old

Something Old represents a bride's ties to her past. It is a symbol of continuity and family. It is an unbreakable connection, an ode to ancestry, a reflection of the love a bride has already been blessed with as a single woman. It is love. It is cherished friendship. It is luck. Whatever object a bride has chosen to represent something old, it is a token that carries meaning behind it. Bridesmaids are family or friends that are like blood. A bridesmaid knows her bride well, and the memories created among her closest friends leave a special imprint on a girl about to be given away. When a bride thinks of her "something old," she's bound to fondly remember the good old days she once spent with her favorite companions/partners in crime.

Paste in a Keepsake
of You and Your
Bridesmaid from the
Good Old Days!

Bridal Beginnings

Number of bridesmaids in the bridal party:

_____

_____

_____

_____

_____

Number of times the bride has been a bridesmaid:

_____

_____

_____

_____

_____

Meet the other bridesmaids:

_____

_____

_____

_____

_____

Meet the flower girl(s):

_____

_____

_____

_____

_____

Meet the mother of the bride:

_____

_____

_____

_____

_____

Meet the mother of the groom:

_____

_____

_____

_____

_____

Welcome to the Bridal Party

Saying yes to becoming a bridesmaid is only the beginning, and there's so much fun and happiness ahead. Sandwiched between the good stuff might be a smidgen of stress. Fear not bridesmaid, just try to remember what it's all about, have a sense of humor, and give the bride a break when she needs a pass. She loves you as a dear friend and knows you will strive to keep her sane through the ups and downs of planning. Buckle up, bridesmaid! Being in the bridal party can feel like a rollercoaster ride, but it's definitely a ticket to a fun experience.

YOU KNOW THE BRIDE BEST

Is the bride a wishy-washy girl or a stern woman with a hard head? Is she often easygoing? You know her best and you probably know what to expect. Just know that sometimes, under these circumstances, she might turn into a basket case. It's no surprise that brides have been known to obsess over decisions related to weddings. It happens to the best of us! After all, there is just so much to consider. On the outside, the bride is picturing a perfect wedding day. On the inside, every strand of sanity is wigging out with uncertainties.

BE THE OTHER ROCK IN THE BRIDE'S LIFE

Now that she has a rock on her finger, a bride could use another constant to hold her up when times get tough. After years of searching for the perfect man, a girl finds herself in search of the perfect dress to wear on a perfect day amidst a perfect bridal party. Except, perfection is a subjective term and often a far-fetched goal. How will a bride ever survive the beautiful madness? Why, with your help, of course! Don't be afraid to laugh at her when she's being a total loon, but don't forget to give her a big hug when she's bottled up too much of her nerves to think straight. A punch in the face might be overkill unless she's become a banshee that needs a reality check from her demonic evolution into a supernatural bridezilla. History tells us the bride is the one to protect—not fear.

HOW MANY BRIDESMAIDS ARE THE NORM?

The term "norm" is really kind of bogus, because every bride, bridal party, and wedding is unique. That being said, more formal weddings tend to have more guests, so a bride in that case might have a larger bridal party consisting of six to twelve bridesmaids. Smaller, more intimate weddings might mean having a smaller bridal party with less than five bridesmaids. There is no right or wrong answer, and whether you are one of two or one of twelve bridesmaids, you are an important piece in this crazy puzzle. You are valued, bridesmaid. Just keep in mind you are one of a group, and that means working together toward the common goal of making this an awesome experience.

WHAT IS EXPECTED OF BRIDESMAIDS?

As a treasured friend, a bridesmaid's job is to make this process fun, easy, and enjoyable for the bride. It's definitely not your job to be her literal maid, and she should know that, so don't be afraid to set her straight if she needs a kick in the rear. The bride's wedding is not a draft where its recruits have no choice but to enlist in all of the planning. Deciding to be a bridesmaid should feel like a mutual agreement, not a binding contract. Seal it with a high five or a hug. Dearest bridesmaid, the bride cares about you and wants you to enjoy this process along with her! She chose you to be in this role. She didn't have to ask, and you didn't have to say yes, but you both did. So, here you are.

BRIDESMAID DUTIES

Saying yes to a bridesmaid proposal means you have agreed to buy a bridesmaid dress. Whether you love it or not, the bride will be counting on you to wear it with a smile. Don't worry, the bride will hopefully take your taste into account! Another part of being a bridesmaid means helping to plan and pay for the bachelorette party and the bridal shower. As a bridesmaid, you are automatically factored into the bill. You will be expected to attend all of the wedding events unless there is some important reason that you cannot make it. If you don't live nearby or have a number of personal conflicts, be sure to discuss this with the bride well before these events are on the calendar so that there aren't any surprises when the time comes. Ultimately, the bridesmaid dress, bachelorette party, and bridal shower are the main to-do's. Other aspects of the wedding planning can be catered to the bride's needs and your own.

HONOR OVER DUTY

It's easy to become overwhelmed or discouraged by the responsibilities that come with being a bridesmaid. Don't think of it as a job, think of it as an honor. Just try to keep in mind what your presence means to your friend about to embark on a wonderful new chapter in her life. Using that vision as a guideline, you should be able to do as little or as much as you see fit. The bride already knows she's asking for a lot. She knows that your schedule might be in disarray because of the events she has planned. She knows your wallet is going to take a hit. She knows you have other responsibilities. Most brides shouldn't need to be reminded of this, but if you feel your bride is forgetting, speak your mind kindly and politely. Humility and a sense of humor are the two great catalysts for happiness and lasting friendship, especially during special yet stressful times like this.

A Special History

This is my fondest memory of our friendship:

_____

_____

_____

_____

_____

This is how we became friends:

_____

_____

_____

_____

_____

Please don't ever let me forget . . .

_____

_____

_____

_____

_____

You were always there for me . . .

_____

_____

_____

_____

_____

I'll always be there for you . . .

_____

_____

_____

_____

_____

This is why I need you now:

_____

_____

_____

_____

_____

Bridesmaid Beginnings

Have you ever wondered how this bridesmaid business ever got started? Today, it's all about bustling the bride's beautiful train (like anyone knows how), holding up the big hoop skirt when a bride can't do it by herself and she really needs to pee (a true mark of friendship), or holding yourself together when everyone else seems to be losing patience (good luck). Speaking of luck, modern brides might lose their minds thinking about the superstitions of former lovebirds. Today, weddings are all about logistics and convenience. Saturdays are the most popular day of the week to wed, with Fridays and Sundays posing more affordable options for frugal couples. Heck, Thursdays are even on the rise. Except, the alleged truth is that Wednesday was once considered the luckiest day of the week to get married. Who knew that it all went downhill after hump day?

Monday for health
Tuesday for wealth
Wednesday best of all
Thursday for losses
Friday for crosses
Saturday for no luck at all

This old folk rhyme sounds like the creation of a bored little girl partaking in a lonely game of hop-scotch. Wednesday is a nice day to wed, because, phonetics? This odd folklore was popular well before the hellish nine-to-five reality that has since chained everyone in the modern world to partying only on the weekends. Turns out modern folks never got the memo about Saturday weddings being a bad idea, or they did and just didn't care because in the real world everybody has some kind of job.

ANCIENT ROMAN LAW

Midweek weddings are best? Wedding guests would either love the excuse to take off from work or they'd miss the party altogether. Hopefully at least ten people would show, because that's how many witnesses were needed to make that vow exchange legit to the ancient Romans. Ancient Rome is where bridesmaids can trace their roots, when the chicks that surrounded the bride were either strongly encouraged or forced by a superstitious hand to dress exactly like the bride! Matching dresses mirroring the bride's motif? Talk about a modern fashion faux pas. Wear white to a wedding? Blasphemous! Off with her head! Ladies today would be crying witch!

A PROTECTIVE BUNCH

It's no joke that bridesmaids of the past were protectors. Ancient folks thought they could derail any demons trying to ruin the bride's happy day by having her girlfriends dress in the same garb. It was imperative to confuse any bad guys lurking near the ceremony grounds by creating identical bride decoys to throw them off. Talk about commitment. A modern girl might wonder how a supernatural entity couldn't see right through the ruse of fabric to find their prey. Though, it is understandable how ten identically dressed women could make anyone buzz off. The bizarre doppelganger effect perhaps worked in a way that raised the crazy ghost initiatives to a new level of crazy that wasn't worth the trouble. Talk about unpaved street smarts from old timers!

THE MAID/MATRON OF HONOR

A bride can decide to have a maid of honor, matron of honor, or both. She also might not have one designated person of honor, though traditionally there is one bridesmaid that leads the pack. A maid of honor is an unmarried bridesmaid and a matron of honor is a married bridesmaid. In Ancient Rome, the matron of honor was thought to be a moral role model for the bride. She was a good wife that was committed to her marriage. She was praised and looked up to for her fidelity and good moral standing.

A BRIDESMAID WITH A MOM PURSE

Married no more than once, the matron of honor's role in the wedding was to join the right hands of the bride and groom for the first time in the ceremony. She was also in charge of the dow-purse and keeping the dowry safe. Luckily (or regrettably, depending on your perspective), this tradition hasn't evolved into the modern matron of honor sporting a tie-dye nineties fanny pack or mom purse filled with cash money. Instead, this special lady only has to worry about holding the bride's bouquet during the ceremony. She is also in charge of making sure that the bride's gown, train, and veil are displayed perfectly to the crowd. She may choose to deliver a poignant toast or speech during the wedding reception. The wedding day is really the icing on the cake, though, as much of the head bridesmaid's duties come well before the wedding.

THE BRIDE'S GO-TO GIRL

During pre-wedding planning, the MOH will be the bride's best sidekick. She will also be in charge of planning the bridal shower and the bachelorette party. That just means facilitating the events, because usually all of the bridesmaids work together to carry the load. It might seem like a lot of work, but it's an honorable job. Somebody has to do it—especially when there are so many good and bad luck superstitions a bride needs to know about!

Ceremonial Superstitions

As the folklore promises, if the bride bears items that represent the traditional good luck suggestions, her marriage will be happy. Not all brides need to be superstitious to have a happy marriage—but why risk it? It's a good thing a bride has some good friends to back her up. Truly, bridesmaids are the best good luck charms a bride could ever need.

SWEET-TOOTH SUPERSTITION

When it comes time to cut the cake, make sure the bride knows she should have a hand in that, especially if the couple wants kiddos. The groom cutting the cake alone symbolizes a marriage void of children. Once the dessert is plated, all guests should have their cake and eat it, too! Some say it's bad luck if a guest refuses a piece of wedding cake. No more sweating for the wedding—time to chow down. Who would complain about such a thing anyway?

BITTERSWEET STAPLE

Jordan almonds have long been a wedding staple, especially at Italian, Middle Eastern, and Greek celebrations. They are a symbol of the bittersweet reality of life, and are often clustered into odd numbers to represent the undivided love of the happy couple. The sugary sweet coating that tops bittersweet tasting almonds is a symbol of hope that the marriage will be more sweet than bitter. Italians often piece the almonds in groups of five, offering five wishes for health, wealth, happiness, children, and a long life.

YOUTHFUL PARTYING SPIRIT

Apparently, evil spirits are kind of like elderly neighbors in that they despise noise. They won't call the police, but they will probably steer clear of the party if the couple rigs noisy cans and other kooky items on the back of their getaway car.

SOULFUL CONNECTION

Middle school kids called it spit swapping, but more mature folks might consider the first kiss between the bride and groom a symbol of soul swapping. In Ancient Rome, it was believed the groom kissed the bride to see if she had been drinking wine. It's uncertain what he would do if she was drinking wine, but a girl could hope he would just give her a smile and a high five.

MIRRORS

It's bad luck for there to be mirrors near the ceremony, and guests should think twice about gifting a mirror. Mirrors break easily, and if they do, it's the seven-year curse. That's like a bad luck whammy and there's already enough things to worry about on a wedding day! Brides should also think twice about checking their entire look in the mirror before the wedding. It's been said doing so could make a bride lose a piece of her soul in her reflection. No bride wants to take soulless selfies! Bridesmaids can help by having a hair clip or extra bobby pin handy, adding a final touch to the bride's getup.

FURRY FRIENDS OR FOES?

Ancient people thought it was good luck to get married under the light of a full moon. They were afraid of ancient spirits but apparently had no worries about werewolves. While a single gal might be afraid of never meeting her soulmate and becoming a cat lady, it turns out cats are pretty lucky for brides and grooms, especially if one's fed soon before the wedding. Sighting a black cat before a wedding is apparently a good omen, too. Of course, not everyone loves cats. Some cultures think seeing certain animals on the way to the wedding ceremony could mean bad luck. Furry creatures to avoid include cats, dogs, and rabbits, while lizards and snakes are equally troublesome for obvious reasons. Maybe the person that made this up just had really bad pet dander, or grew tired of watching animated princesses unrealistically burst into forest songs with small animals.

EIGHT LEGS OF LUCK

Creepy crawlers aren't so bad. In fact, when it comes to getting married, spiders are like the popular kid everyone wants at their sweet sixteen party to prove it's legit. Spiders symbolize happiness, so if one finds its way onto a bride's wedding dress, she should jump with joy, not fear. Could it be that humans have had it wrong this whole time? Is everyone just afraid of happiness because it walks on eight legs? EEK! Happiness! Quick! Get a man in here to kill it!

RISKY BRIDESMAID BUSINESS

A bridesmaid falling in love with a wedding guest is okay, but falling down on her way to the altar means she might never marry. Bridesmaids should wear shoes fit for dancing and take care to put one foot in front of the other. Maybe save the bulk of the champagne binging for the dance floor after the "I do's," when standing up straight isn't as much of a life or death situation.

BRIDESMAID HAT TRICK

The old saying, "Three times a bridesmaid, never a bride," suggests that if a girl can't land a man after dressing up three times, she's doomed to be a single lady forever. Seems like unfair logic, since bridesmaid dresses aren't known for being all that cute. History likes to say a serial bridesmaid must be tainted with evil after acting as a shield against darkness to protect other brides so many times. On the bright side, imagine the strength and independence of a professional bridesmaid! Who knows if getting married is even on her to-do list, but if it is, any dude would be lucky to have her by his side. She's the type of woman that fears nothing when battling darkness to protect love, and she has a closet full of bridesmaid dresses to prove it.

THAT WISHY-WASHY RAIN CLOUD

There's a bit of a disagreement among cultures about rain and weddings. Some say it's good luck, others say it's bad luck, often with the same reasoning behind their beliefs. One person is over here stressing that a rainy wedding day means so many more tears to come! Another person is over there smiling that a rainy wedding day means no more tears to come! Some whine that a rainy wedding day is a foreshadowing of a stormy, sad life. Others believe it represents the last tears the bride and groom will shed as a couple, therefore embarking on a happy life together under a cloudy sky. In other words, it can only get better from there.

THE BRIGHT SIDE

Is the glass half empty or half full? They say a bride who marries on a rainy day will have a stormy marriage. Big deal. The bride should redirect that mantra to find stormy excitement in the bedroom. Some mountain people think that rain on a wedding day means a bride will become a bad housewife. If that's not an excuse to get out of cooking and cleaning, what is? Sounds like a great escape route to the shoe store.

THE BRIDAL BABY MAKER

The biggest consensus seems to be that rain should be welcomed and celebrated because it represents fertility and cleansing, a washing away of past sorrows as newlyweds embark on a happy future of sunshine. There was also some alleged bride that gave birth to a beautiful baby exactly nine months after her wedding day, which, of course, was a rainy one.

WEATHERING A LIFETIME OF LOVE

Rain or shine, a wedding day is really just how a couple and a group of people view what life throws at them. Those that want to sulk, may sulk. Those that want to make the best of what they cannot control, such as weather, may find themselves dancing in the rain and celebrating love. Making the best of it is a great lesson to learn on the first day of marriage.

MAKING YOUR OWN LUCK

Not all brides need to be superstitious to have a happy marriage—but why risk it? It's a good thing a bride has some good friends to back her up. Truly, the bridesmaids are the best good luck charms a bride could ever need.

QUIZ

Bridesmaid,
How Well Do You Know the Bride?

Who did the bride want to marry when she was a little girl? _____

What was the bride's favorite childhood hobby? _____

Where was the bride born? _____

When did the bride realize you were awesome? _____

Note: see the bride's answers to these questions on pg. 79!

An Old Experience

Good for: _____

Use by: _____

Something New

Something New represents the new life a bride is embarking on after she walks down the aisle. It is the anticipation of a life filled with love and happiness. It is a symbol of hope for the future. It is love. It is the evolution of friendship. It is luck. Friendships honored in a bridal party are not flighty, passing, or gone with the turning of a new page into married life. The ink of camaraderie is not easily erased from a bride's longtime book of love. Remember all of the other new chapters and challenges when friendship was the constant? Before a bride met her soul mate, she counted on her soul sisters to get her through moments when her own confidence and strength was not enough. It's not just the wedding day that a bride needs the support of her closest friends. It's the new, the ever after, too. A bride's vision of a future filled with love and happiness would not be complete without the companionship of old friends.

Paste in a Keepsake
of You and Your
Bridesmaid from
a Challenge You
Overcame!

The Bachelorette Party

Women's independence and liberation aren't only accepted today, they are encouraged and saluted like no other time in history. Modern gals can walk into a store and decide whether or not they want to toast to their singlehood with penis straws and pink tiaras. Appreciating the fact that most modern cultures allow groups of women to gallivant around town in celebration of a bride's one true love doesn't mean all bridesmaids need to go to the nines and blow the whole thing out of proportion. That is up to the bridesmaids leading (or stumbling) the way forward. Of course, not every woman needs a symbolic night of debauchery to celebrate the last days of her singlehood, but that doesn't mean it's not a rite of passage for others. Being born with the right to choose might make some brides naive to the reality that not too long ago, bachelorette parties (or hen dos, as they are called across the pond) weren't much of a thing.

IT'S A PARTY NO MATTER WHAT YOU CALL IT

In the United States and Canada, it's known as a bachelorette party. In the United Kingdom and Ireland, it's known as a hen party, hen do, or hen night. A hen party? Seriously? Before it had anything to do with marriage, the term hen party sprung up in the late 1800s in reference to a bunch of girls cackling and chitchatting about whatever it was they cared about back then—probably washboards and girdles. Back in the 1600s, some unlucky broad was the first to be referred to as a hen, and men haven't forgotten, making jokes about the cackling hens in the kitchen. It's the Victorian-era equivalent of being the first chick to be called a grenade.

KEEPING UP WITH THE BOYS

Brides have come a long way from being captured to being traded for goods to having a say in whether or not a boyfriend has the goods to become a longtime love. The evolution of the pre-vow celebration paints a cultural picture of gender equality. It's hard to believe that women weren't fighting to jump on the pre-wedding party bandwagon sooner, considering age-old Spartans were the first dudes to realize their stag parties were an epic idea back in the 5th century BC. Spartan grooms would feast and chill with their best buds over dinner the night before the wedding, bidding farewell to the good-old single Spartan days and welcoming in the co-ed life of marriage. The closest thing chicks had to that predates the Spartans in Ancient Greece, when brides presented childhood belongings and even locks of their hair to the gods in a pre-wedding ceremony sacrifice. Such pre-wedding ceremonies wouldn't fly today. Could you imagine a worse time to try out a new trendy hair cut? Baby bangs? Please. It would be like high school yearbook fails all over again. The bachelorette party tradition didn't gain steam until much later when women started tossing preconceived notions of their societal roles out the little windows above their kitchen sinks! Once attitudes about female sexuality and marital roles changed in the sixties, soon-to-be brides took their drinking cups and ran with them—straight to the bar. Who could blame them?

TROUSSEAU TROPHIES

Hen parties gained fame during the days of Charles II of England, when the bride and her female friends would get together to inspect the bride's bottom drawer or trousseau. Trousseau sounds super fancy and legit, as all historical references should. Back then, women didn't feel a need to have a final fling. A girl spent her days pining away, hoping her dream mate would choose her and take her as his wife. As a result, all that pining led to her hoping and her parents hoarding items for her wedded future.

HOPE CHEST HOEDOWNS

In Victorian England, a wealthy bride would have hosted a party to show off her trousseau items, and could you blame her? She was all, "Look at me, look at me," while showing off her one-of-a-kind linens. Apparently, one of the most beloved pieces of trousseau was the bridal handkerchief, which was doused with perfume and rubbed on the bride's face, then hung on her shoulders and neck. Seems like a poor option for a quality complexion, but who knows? They didn't have fried foods back then so maybe adult acne wasn't a thing. Anyway, it was more of a rich girl to-do for a while, and then eventually evolved to include poor chicks that were also interested in the hope chest game. Originally called the trousseau, more modern versions were called hope chests, dowry chests, and even glory boxes.

MY DAUGHTER'S DOWRY DRAWERS

In American colonial times, a young girl's bottom drawer (get your mind out of the gutter) was all the rage with her parents' predictions of what she would need to be marketed to an eligible suitor for marriage. *My Daughter's Dowry Drawers* could be an award-winning reality TV show today. It was common for a chick to have a collection of items that were meant to help her become a good wife and embark on a happy life in wedlock. Hope chests were truly pretty awesome because the bridal accessories inside were all handmade linens. Today, handmade items cost a fortune, but back then it was a family heirloom that meant something. More recent attempts to recreate the magic of the trousseau often devolve into some sort of laughable internet crafting fail.

Modern-Day Party Planning

From glory boxes to glory days, each bride has to determine whether she's a traditional handkerchief girl or a modern girl with clear pores before deciding what kind of pre-wedding extravaganza she really desires. That decision-making process is where modern-day bridesmaids play a major role. The maid of honor will likely take charge when it comes to planning the ultimate send-off to a sister about to tie the knot with her soul mate. That doesn't mean other bridesmaids aren't invited to play a big part in brainstorming. Keep in mind this whole event should be built around what you think the bride values and how she wants to celebrate with her friends. It's okay to run things by her, communicate, and ask for help. Let her be your guide, but don't be afraid to kindly keep her expectations in check if her ideas are a little too extravagant.

PERSONALIZING THE PARTY

Whereas one bride might want to drink her face off, another might want to slap some mud on her face and get a manicure. Other brides might want to sweat out the toxins before slurping them down. Every bride is different: some are low-key and picture a simple night out on the town or a chick flick marathon, while others envision a weeklong vacation with their best buds—a last hoorah that requires a plane ride and some sunblock. It really all comes down to preference—and budget.

DECIDING ON A BUDGET

While money might not be a big deal for one bridesmaid, it might be nonexistent for another, which can make planning pricey suggestions taxing on a group's mojo. Bridal parties can avoid hurt feelings by discussing what they are comfortable spending well ahead of time. Individuals should not be afraid to kindly and politely profess an opinion about what price point is possible for their financial situation.

CHOOSING THE RIGHT HOST

The bride should designate a people-pleasing troop leader that will motivate, inspire, and think outside the box. The bride might want to be very involved in the planning of her own party, or she might want to be totally surprised. Ultimately, her level of involvement is her own choice. She might even want to host her own party. If not, the bridal party should communicate what makes sense for who takes the lead on the planning. It might be a family member or the maid/matron of honor that hosts the extravaganza, but really it could be any friend that's willing.

COMMUNICATING IDEAS

Splitting up various responsibilities among the group can help everyone feel involved and valued. Keep the girl talk friendly, supportive, and productive! It's common courtesy to let guests know well ahead of time when a party is scheduled so that they can plan their lives around it. Bridesmaids should waste no time in saving a date to celebrate. Once that's on the calendar, don't worry so much about sending out snail mail. That's a viable option, but email and social media are a modern girl's best friend when it comes to saving some dough better spent on drinks.

INVITING THE BRIDE'S FRIENDS & FAMILY

While a wedding guest list can range from an intimate thirty folks to a more elaborate three-hundred, bachelorette parties don't need to mirror those numbers. In fact, bachelorette party etiquette doesn't really require that every attendee be a wedding guest. If they aren't, it's just important that those people know they might not be on the wedding list. A bride just needs to genuinely tell people why certain things might be happening. For example, a bride that's having a small wedding or a destination wedding might want to invite the girlfriends that didn't make the cut for the big day to her bachelorette party so that she can still celebrate with them.

DECIDING ON A THEME

When it comes to throwing an awesome party, it comes down to the personality of the person the party is meant to honor. Bridesmaids are the fabric of a bride's former life, current life, and future life as a wife. They know her best. They know her likes and dislikes, her hobbies and habits. All of this knowledge can be used to design a heartfelt celebration that matches the bride's traits and enhances her love of life. The most important thing to remember is that the bride wants to have fun and she wants her guests to enjoy this time spent together. Keep an open mind and a humble heart, and be ready to bend for the dance-offs and decision-making.

Bachelorette Party
& Bridal Shower

This is my favorite memory of you at a party:

_____

_____

_____

_____

_____

This is what I think a bachelorette party is about:

_____

_____

_____

_____

This is what I expect from you at my party:

_____

_____

_____

_____

If I could shower you with five things for life, they would be . . .

_____

_____

_____

_____

_____

This is what I hope for my bridal shower:

_____

_____

_____

_____

_____

If I could give you one gift, it would be . . .

_____

_____

_____

_____

The Bridal Shower

Did you ever encounter a comical friend in primary school that insisted they were only friends with you because your parents were paying them to pretend? Did you ever wonder if they were just joking around, or if they were the first frenemy you ever had? Do you remember those sorority jokes about buying your friends? It's disheartening to think that relationships might be bartered with bank accounts. If you think such bribes are rubbish, just think about the brides of the past whose families needed to present dowries or payments to the groom's family before their nuptials.

DOWRIES

How would a girl know if a guy really loved her, or if he was just after her (hope) chest? Were daisies around back then? Sounds like a whole lot of *he loves me, he loves me not* being played in the middle of beautiful pastures. A dowry is a gift of money or property brought from the bride to the groom in exchange for their marriage. It's interesting to think about, but the bridal showers of today might owe their existence to the days of dowries. The practice of a bride's family providing a dowry is one of the oldest bridal traditions and was definitely taking place long before people even started calling them such (or speaking English); American colonial hope chests kept a similar tradition alive even after the traditional dowry was outdated. These hope boxes contained items that made a bride look pretty darn good to the groom, helping her bait an eligible suitor and convince his family she had all of the right stuff. (And they say women are gold diggers . . ..) Anyway, back when marriages seemed to be less about love and more about making a good deal, there's a legend that offers some fairy tale hope to the hearts of romantics.

AN OLD-SCHOOL ROM-COM SET IN SOME DUTCH VILLAGE

Holla back at 16th century Holland, when dowries were every dame's game and marrying rich was a hot ticket to a good life. Of course, every individual has her own idea of what marrying rich means. As the story goes, there was this high society Dutch girl that was making googly eyes at the wrong boy from the other side of the tracks, or stream . . . whatever. It was wrong in the eyes of her cranky-pants father. The girl was in love with the village grain-miller's son, a remarkably selfless guy.

Her father was stubborn and had his sights set on a richer ticket. He thought the miller was low-class, poor, and unfit to be given a dowry. This had rom-com fame written all over it.

AN ANCIENT UNDERRATED DREAMBOAT

Literally, the entire community saw this bachelor for what he was: a giver trying to make the village a better place by feeding the hungry and giving out his bread and flour at no cost to those that couldn't afford to pay. Maybe the dad saw a future filled with his daughter living in a shanty, and maybe the dad wasn't wrong. Who knows? But in the grand tradition of true love stories, the girl was committed to the forbidden boy. This guy seemed to be the bleeding heart type that would have given the shirt off his back and the food from his own plate if he thought it would have made a dime of a difference to someone else. Let's imagine he had a nineties flattop haircut, too. Swoon!

ALL ABOUT THAT BACON

Naturally, everyone that came into contact with this do-gooder adored him. Except, Dutch girl's daddy was a stubborn old man that refused her dowry to this dreamboat kid. The father insisted that his daughter marry some overweight pig farmer with a lot of pigs and even more money. It's unknown if the father had ever tried a pork roll sandwich, because if he envisioned that, who could have blamed him for acting so brash? Papa Bear might have just had a craving. Everyone loves bacon, but still, a man has to draw the line somewhere. Anyway, the bride's father threatened her with no dowry if she didn't marry the man of his choosing. As all rom-com fairy tales go, the girl obviously went with her gut, deciding what marrying rich meant to her, which was poor in the pocket but full in the heart.

GIRLS RUN THE WORLD

As a result, all of this chick's girlfriends ran out of their village huts throwing gifts at the bride, presumably while dancing to some upbeat pop song about female empowerment. Imagine, all of the village ladies jamming out to Beyoncé's "Run the World (GIRLS)!" It would be a classic throwback music video set in a legit town where girls took the power of love into their own hands. "Who run the world? GIRLS!" Maybe that's not exactly how it all went down, but you get the gist. The bride's friends got together and presented her with gifts in place of the dowry, in the name of love. Apparently, the dad's heart wasn't made of ice or stone because the selflessness of the groom, his daughter, and their loved ones convinced him to accept and support the marriage. Ever since this story sort of happened, friends shower the bride with gifts before the wedding. Though, oddly enough, bacon hasn't made its way into the tradition of crafting cute bridal baskets, but it honestly probably should.

WHY IS IT CALLED A SHOWER?

The shower piece-of-the-pie might reference a lady from the 1800s who decided it would be a great idea to put a bunch of little gifts into a parasol (dainty umbrella), then shower them over the bride's head to literally mimic showering the bride with gifts. Sources suggest this as a point of origin, leaving readers questioning if the bride in that case was excited or enraged. What kind of woman wants a friend to dump gifts over her head? What if someone bought the lady a knife set? What then? It's actually considered bad luck to buy newlyweds knife sets as a gift, so if you do, make sure they give you a penny or some form of payment to avoid a broken relationship later. Gifts are meant to be softly handed to the recipient, not barbarically dumped on them like some ancient drunkard. If a bridesmaid tried dumping today's gifts over the bride's head, the woman of the hour might end up with a concussion, benching her from dancing at her own wedding. Her swollen brain would be out of whack and she wouldn't be able to get jiggy with it on the dance floor or pass out after the fact. She'd become a zombie bride and all of the pictures the couple spent so much money on would collect dust for years because the bride's state of confusion would force her eyes closed or crossed in the flash of the photographer's camera. This is all hypothetical paranoia, but it's definitely something to think about. After all, blenders and toasters are heavy and only meant to bang the heads of home-intruders. The umbrellas are cute for decoration, but bridesmaids should leave it at that!

Bridal Showers Today

Like the bachelorette party, bridal showers are typically hosted by the bridesmaids. However, a bride's mother might choose to take charge of the event, too. Bridal showers are essentially chick fests that enable women to buy the bride all of the awesome goodies she'll need to set up her house in legit fashion. It's usually a women-only event limited to wedding guests, however some couples may opt to have a Jack and Jill shower that opens the doors to dudes as well.

PLANNING THE SHOWER

The shower is typically held within three months of the wedding, a kickoff to all of the other awesome things approaching on a bride's timeline. It should be discussed with the bride whether or not she would prefer the shower to be a surprise. Some brides might not want to know a thing about this! Others may request a location, share a guest list, or suggest an idea to aid the planning process. While bridesmaids are in charge of the planning, the end result should ultimately be about what the bride prefers and requests. As long as the bride is polite and reasonable without being a microman-ager, her involvement shouldn't be much of an issue. This event is about her life as a wife, after all.

DECIDING ON A BUDGET

Just as the bridesmaids shell out dough for the bachelorette party, they have a financial obligation to help pay for the shower unless someone else says she will be taking care of all of the expenses. Sometimes the bride's family will decide to pay for the shower. However, that is not to be assumed. The typical scenario is that bridesmaids will host the party. Because of that, the group should dis-cuss early on what they would like to budget for the shower. Once everyone knows what they are able to spend, the organizer can help facilitate an appropriate hosting location.

CHOOSING A SETTING

Some brides may prefer the intimate yet casual setting of a home belonging to a close friend or family member. Others might opt for the formality of a sit-down restaurant. Whereas one choice might involve decorating and coordinating a caterer or cooking food, another choice might involve more money and less legwork. The time of day can range from a late morning brunch to an evening dinner. While time, location, and other choices can be made according to what is convenient for the entire party, the final priority should be about making the bride happy. This event is about showering the bride with unconditional love. Once the time and location are selected, food and drink decisions can follow.

PICKING A THEME

Not every great party needs a theme, but having one certainly doesn't hurt. This is the fun part. The theme could fit with something personal about the bride, or it could be a guiding color or idea that makes the entire day a cohesive event. Don't be afraid to delegate responsibilities, and be understanding if one bridesmaid has less time to commit to planning than others. Different women might be at different stages in their lives and have varying personal responsibilities. Working together to arrange the food, drinks, games, and decorations is much easier than putting all of that stuff on one person's plate. That one bridesmaid would be full of the responsibility and need a serious nap!

QUIZ

Bridesmaid,
How Well Do You Know the Bride?

Who would play the bride in a movie? _____

What is the bride's favorite hobby as an adult? _____

Where did the bride meet the groom? _____

When did the bride say YES to the groom? _____

Note: see the bride's answers to these questions on pg. 79!

A New Experience

Good for: _____

Use by: _____

Something Borrowed

Something Borrowed represents friendship. Brides might borrow a veil, hairclip, or a vintage hand-bag to accompany their big day and fulfill the third piece of the old English poem. It is often said that this symbol brings the best luck to the bride if she has borrowed the item from another happily married couple or a former bride that was blessed by a successful marriage. No one really speaks on whether borrowing a beautiful piece of jewelry from a divorcée is going to put the hex on anything. It is really about borrowing happiness, so the bride should choose which person has more than enough of that emotion to go around. It is love. It is joy and friendship shared. It is luck. A bride is blessed when she can look at her bridal party and recall many times before when she has borrowed happiness from a bridesmaid.

Paste in a Keepsake
of the Happiest
Memory Shared with
Your Bridesmaid!

Finding the One

Saying yes to the man she loves is just the first of many big decisions in the bride-to-be's life. Modern culture insists she must say yes to a dress, too. Not every bride will want to carry her entire entourage with her to bridal shops like a chapel train that's laced with varying opinions that might confuse her own. Some brides crave the feedback and attention, while others might be intimidated by the fuss and the price tags. Whatever type of shopper she is, the bride has a great deal to think about. Does she hope to show off her curves or cap her classy innocence? Will she opt to dress as everyone expects or choose a look more daring and unique? You know her best, and you may have borrowed a thing or two from her closet in years past. What do you think?

A BORROWED EXPERIENCE

Perhaps the family excitement surrounding picking a wedding dress stems from the days when weddings felt more like a business deal. Back then, brides wore dresses that represented the family in the best light. Maybe that's where all of the outspoken opinions from the bride's peanut gallery can trace their critical roots. The idea of everyone trucking down to the store together is a nice way to share the experience, but it might not be what every bride has in mind. Sometimes a bride wants to bring her bridesmaids, too, but don't be offended if your bride chooses to fly solo. The best thing a bridesmaid could do is provide feedback when requested and help when possible.

A BORROWED IDEA

Queen Victoria is largely given credit for being the bride that sparked the white wedding dress tradition, but the first documented case of a chick donning white on her big day was when Anne of Brittany married Louis XII of France in 1499. Mary, Queen of Scots, also wore white in 1558. Still, it wasn't until 1840 when Queen Victoria married her cousin, Prince Albert of Saxe-Coburg and Gotha that girls started gossiping about how wedding gowns just had to be white. No one seemed to care about the cousin thing because they were too fascinated by the beauty of the dress, and it wasn't as weird back then. Anyway, finding inspiration from Queen V, an American women's magazine declared white to be the go-to shade of bridal fashion. Then, women everywhere borrowed the idea and began losing their minds over showing off their social status and wealth.

AN INNOCENT EXPRESSION

Back when dry cleaning wasn't on the corner of every street, only wealthy women could really afford to wear white because the light color was difficult to obtain and preserve. Less fortunate families realized it made no sense to spend a ton of time making a white dress that would still be dirty after washing it. There were no Tide pens back then. So, rather than invest in a dress they could only wear once, they wore the best dress they could find in their closet. After the Great Depression and during the second half of the 20th century, the color white was no longer a symbol of wealth or status because of sewing innovations. Thankfully for the middle class, white became a popular wedding dress choice again for everyday women. It became a symbol of purity and virtue as it grew in popularity.

A CLOSET FULL OF STYLE

The main styles seen in bridal gowns and bridesmaid dresses are A-line, ball gown, mermaid, empire waist, drop waist, trumpet, and sheath. You might have an idea of what you think the bride will look best in, but try to remember that the bride has her own vision of what she hopes to accomplish in her look. This is the one dress in the bride's wardrobe a friend won't be borrowing anytime soon. Try not to force your opinions on her, but provide feedback when appropriate. If she is in love with a dress that looks nice, but you don't love it, you can tell her it's not your favorite, but it's still beautiful. If a dress looks absolutely terrible on the bride, and she hasn't purchased it yet, it's okay to voice your opinion so long as you do so kindly. If she already bought the dress, maybe keep your disappointments in her selection to yourself. Criticism works best when it's delivered with thought, sensitivity, and compassion. It's okay to let the bride know what silhouette you feel most comfortable in for the bridesmaid dress you're being forced to wear, but also understand she hopefully will do her best to accommodate your needs along with the requests of everyone else in the group.

MORE THAN A SILHOUETTE

A-line and empire waist dresses are the most universally flattering because the cut works on a variety of body types. As a result, these two styles are often very common for bridesmaids if everyone is wearing the same cut. Whoever coined the term A-line wasn't messing around, because these dresses legitimately make the shape of an A on a person's body, and they work for all kinds of figures. Hence receiving an A+ from every bride when thinking about bridesmaid dress styles. Empire waist gowns have a high-waist that falls just below the bust line, drawing the eye away from the waistline and the hips to emphasize the whole body as a lean, evil spirit–fighting bridesmaid machine.

Ball gowns are built for women aiming to feel like princesses, though all bridesmaids should feel like princesses no matter what. Ball gowns are romantic, fun, and timeless. Dropped waist gowns offer similar glam with a little less volume. A sheath gown is simple and formfitting but still ever so elegant and classic. Mermaid gowns hug the body and then flare out at the bottom. Regardless of the name, they don't help you swim better in the ocean, nor do trumpet gowns make you more musically inclined. Similar to mermaids, trumpet styles also have a straighter bodice that slightly flares at the bottom. Either way, both gowns hopefully inspire a bridesmaid to dance and party the night away without ending up face down in a pool or singing inebriated karaoke in front of two hundred people.

MORE THAN A DRESS

It doesn't matter how good you look in your dress. You are probably never going to wear it again. It's sad to say, but it's a one and done deal. Bridesmaid dresses are the one-hit-wonders of the wedding circuit. There's no album, just one song that sounds like a broken record if it's pulled out of the closet again. The investment doesn't have to be a total bummer. Just because you forgot to dry clean your pale blush chiffon gown despite the many wine stains that littered the bodice doesn't mean you need to completely trash it as a lost cause. First, you should congratulate yourself on having had a pretty awesome night—a dirty dress is the best sign of that. Second, you should put on your thinking cap and consider what you could possibly do with the fabric that wasn't ruined.

A DIFFERENT OUTLET

Maybe you won't wear your dress again for real, but what about for Halloween as a high school prom queen or zombie princess? Or, you could have a prom party with your best girlfriends, because, why not play dress up again? It's fun. You could wear it while you make dinner, or you could shorten the hemline to make it more casual. You could donate it, dye it, or destroy it. Think about how much fun it is to destroy a pair of stockings. You notice a tiny rip in the transparent tights, then tug at the miniscule hole throughout the day. All of a sudden, the garment has been annihilated to shreds. It feels like a weird accomplishment. An underwear's coming-of-age story. Your dress served its purpose. Why not have a little fun in sending it off to fabric heaven?

A REBIRTH OF FABRIC

If you can't sew, you might want to learn how, because you could reuse your dress fabric to make princess dresses for your kids' dolls in the future. Or you could make your daughter a princess dress—she'd probably love that. You could make a statement pillow for your apartment. You could craft a quilt out of all of the bridesmaid dresses you have accumulated over the years. Pieces of the dress might be a cute way to accent picture frames or scrap books. Maybe you could compile a wedding scrapbook that features all of your friends' weddings, including pictures of you with different brides and a piece of each dress to document your dedication.

A NEW PERSPECTIVE

If you're still not sure what to do, why not collaborate with other bridesmaids and have a yard sale during prom season at someone's house? The key is to think outside of the box and utilize all of the resources out there to find ways to do something with this dress. You wore it. You bought it. You own it! It doesn't have to die in a closet—it can be reborn as something fabulous.

Sharing More Than Memories

If I could borrow anything from your closet, I'd choose . . .

_____

_____

_____

_____

_____

If I could borrow any of your talents or features, I'd choose . . .

_____

_____

_____

_____

_____

I am most proud of being your friend because . . .

_____

_____

_____

_____

_____

This is an accessory I can't live without:

_____

_____

_____

_____

_____

If you were a fabric or accessory, you would be . . .

_____

_____

_____

_____

_____

I feel confident standing next to you because . . .

_____

_____

_____

_____

_____

Bridal Accessories

Sometimes the right accessory can take a girl's look to new heights. Some say less is more. Others might think more is never enough. Whether a bride's approach to dressing up is simple in the details or extravagant around the edges, she should aim to stay true to herself. Nobody wants to look like someone else on their wedding day. If a bride doesn't normally go for large pieces of jewelry, she might feel out of her element walking around with an overpowering amulet choking her neck. Dearest bridesmaid, you can help her stay true to who she is while encouraging her to express herself in new ways that make her shine bright. After all, accessorizing is the fun part. Flowers, bouquets, veils, shoes, jewelry, and garter belts are like everything else related to weddings—they come with stories!

SMELLS LIKE ANCIENT SPIRIT

Flowers have always had a place in weddings, and bridesmaids young and old have always carried beautiful bouquets. They're a visually stunning addition to décor and bring forth an equally pleasant, memorable aroma. Except, flowery scents were not enough when herbal essences were a product of nature and not a shampoo that inspired seductive shower singing. Back when dark forces were a hot wedding topic, ancient brides incorporated bundles of garlic and other potent herbs into a bridesmaid's bouquet. An ancient bride's besties would carry bundles of herby stench to deter mean ghouls and distract guests that were unfortunately ghosted by a bridesmaid's smelly armpits in passing. No bridesmaid wanted her own body odor to dissuade guests from positively gasping at the beauty of the bride on her big day. Passing out due to heat? Okay. Passing out because a bridesmaid was a skunk? Not okay.

FLOWERY ROOTS

Bouquets toted by bridesmaids in the early 1900s looked like something they pulled out of the forest on their way to the altar. Pieces of stems trickled down from the bunch like they were soul-searching for their roots. They were spectacular, just kind of huge, and would probably serve less intense brides better hanging somewhere on the front porches of their homes. Nowadays, it's not crazy to see non-traditional brides break the flower pot mold and try something new in the bridesmaid bouquet department. Trendy alternatives such as baskets, lanterns, corsages, purses, and even vintage fans are finding their way into the hands of bridesmaids as they walk down the aisle.

FLOWER GIRLS

Flower girls were equally dependable when it came to ceremonial ghostbusting. While cute brides-maids-in-training adorably sprinkle flower petals down the aisle, just know that they too are offering the bride some padding between the epic ceremony she is having on Earth and the dark forces potentially brewing beneath the surface. Plus, a young girl's virginity was a shield against the devil. Flower girls got their start in Ancient Rome and Greece when they sprinkled clusters of herbs and wheat as good-vibe offerings to the bride. With wishes of fertility and prosperity, flower girls have always been cute-as-can-be additions to the bridal party, and even once used stinky garlic to tell those mean, evil ghosts to get lost.

WEDDING VEIL

Modern ladies still have the tradition of wearing a veil, which predates the wedding dress. During medieval times and even today, it is considered a symbol of virginity, innocence, and purity. In Ancient Rome, the veil likely began as another scare tactic to ward off evil ghosts. Even if it seems like all of the ancient wedding crashers came from another dimension, there were humans to fear, too. A groom could avoid being killed by any raging lunatics interested in the bride's bod if her beauty was concealed. In the days of arranged marriages, the veil also helped shield the bride's looks from the groom so that he had no time to change his mind as she stepped closer to the altar, in case he didn't like what he saw. While looks weren't everything, some grooms weren't about to "take" a bride they couldn't flaunt around like a proud trophy, and families of the bride weren't about to risk it. Arranged marriages were kind of like modern-day car sales. Veils were the waxed exterior or the new paint job, and the bride's family needed to lock up that wedding arrangement whether the bride's beauty came from within (or she was without). Wearing a paper bag with eye slits over her head wouldn't have inspired the same timeless glamour as the veil, plus the groom would have known something was up.

LIFTING THE VEIL

Lifting the bride's veil is symbolic of a bride leaving her father's house and starting anew with her spouse. The father of the bride lifting the veil is a delicate gesture of him giving his daughter away to another. It's like a sweet signal that kind of suggests she can go off and make her husband sandwiches now. The groom lifting the veil from the bride's face is a nod to his male dominance and power over her. It's like he is unwrapping his little mummy present to keep forever as his toy. If a bride lifts the veil herself, she wears the pants in the relationship! Actually, her lifting the veil just symbolizes her independence and equality, and an independent woman can wear whatever she wants. That is, unless she has a job with a dress code. Then she has to follow the dress code. Otherwise, every woman would probably walk around barefoot in yoga pants—or no pants at all.

BEEKEEPER BRIDES

While the veil comes from a place of protection from evil, if worn today, it makes a classic statement exuding elegance and grace. It's hard not to notice that some of them look more like beekeeper get-ups than anything else, but they are definitely on trend. Speaking of bugs, the veil offers a different, more practical kind of protection to outdoor brides that prefer the rustic theme that has become all the rage in modern-day wedding planning. When the exchanging of vows takes place near some kind of rural river venue, a bride is going to need some sort of shield to repel the kamikaze gnats and mosquitoes from diving into her eyeballs. A bride should not waste tears on bugs and should only cry in happiness on her big day. A pretty veil can do the trick.

VEILS, HATS, AND HEADPIECES

There was a time when bridesmaids wore veils, too! Back when they all dressed like the bride, and even after that. The long wedding veils of the early 1900s were often made of lace and tulle, and usually the bride wore some kind of floral headpiece beneath the veil to accent it. Headpieces became more like a whole head a decade later, and a bridesmaid might be seen wearing a giant hat that appeared to weigh as much as her entire body. The next two decades brought flapper styles and short bobbed haircuts, which meant women felt compelled to cover their skulls with little Juliet caps that looked like they could double as swim gear. It was aquatic chic. Brides in the 1940s had their bridesmaids wearing shorter veils along with them, often of the shoulder length or birdcage variety. The fifties and sixties brought bigger veils with more oomph to match the full skirts on trend. It was like a hairstyle on top of a hairstyle. The seventies were more about hats and all of that hippy love. The eighties went big to match the teased hair, and the nineties were about choosing whatever look the bride liked. Since then, a bride can track down any veil she wants online. Oh, the freedom of searching the net for tulle netting!

IF THE SHOE FITS

Women are funny in that we tend to crave every pair of shoes on the planet, yet can't wait to slip our poor piggies out of them after a long night of dancing. It turns out having a crush on shoes is not just a modern-day shopping obsession. It might be written in our DNA to want and need all of the shoes as human beings with fashion sense. In fact, different cultures put great emphasis on receiving shoes as gifts in the wedding world. A number of countries have ancient beliefs about shoes being a symbol of luck. It was common for some bridegrooms to present their brides with a new pair of shoes as a wedding gift. In some places, it was even a gift presented to family members! A Finnish or Greek mother-in-law would be hard-pressed to let her daughter marry any dude until she was handed a new pair of pumps.

SHOE SUPERSTITIONS

On the other side of the coin, it's also been said that a bride that wears an old pair of shoes to the wedding will be lucky. Sounds like a superstition one of those former shoe-buying bridegrooms invented to deter future women from needing a new pair. (What better excuse to buy a new pair of fancy shoes than a girl's wedding day?) Whatever shoes she has on, a bride should probably take them off during the first dance. It's considered unlucky to groove to the first wedding dance with her shoes on!

THROWING SHOES

In Anglo-Saxon times, a bride's dad would give the groom one of her shoes so that the groom could nudge her head with the sole of it, apparently showcasing his authority. That sort of tactic might inspire a more modern bride to kick the groom with the heel of her other shoe, but who knows? Back then, the bride was doing some shoe-throwing of her own. She'd toss her shoe at the bridesmaids and whichever one caught the darn thing would marry next! Then, that bridesmaid would throw a shoe at a group of men to find out which one of them was about to get hitched. Bridesmaids that didn't feel like catching or dodging shoes being thrown at them could have just found an old pair of boots. There's a belief that doing so could be a foreshadowing of engagement.

BRIDESMAID SHOES

Every bride is different and some might hope their bridesmaids look cohesive with the same pair of shoes. Oftentimes the bride will just request a certain shade of sandal or heel so that the group blends. In an era of mix-and-match or mismatched bridesmaid dresses, wearing the same exact shoe as other bridesmaids could tie the whole look together. Bridesmaids attending outdoor weddings on grassy knolls should consider wedge heels, chunky heels, or no heels. Style is of importance but not as much as comfort. Ideally, a bridesmaid would find a little bit of both and be able to rock the night away without painfully grabbing for her ankles in the corner.

JEWELRY

Sometimes a bride's gift to her bridesmaids is jewelry. This isn't a given, but it's a popular choice. Before the wedding, it might be a good idea to check in with the bride to see what style jewelry she would like everyone to wear. Maybe everyone is wearing silver, gold, or some kind of pearls. Keep in mind you want to accent your look without overpowering the bride's look. Anything that's a statement piece should really receive the bride's stamp of approval.

QUIZ

Bridesmaid, How Well Do You Know the Bride?

Bridesmaids really are the ultimate accessory to a bride's overall look on her big day. The collection of personalities, bright smiles, and good humor are the glowing accents that help her become the brightest version of herself on a day when all eyes will be on her and the groom.

Whose wardrobe does the bride want to raid? _____

What material item can the bride not live without? _____

Where does the bride love to shop? _____

When did/will she know the dress is *the one*? _____

Note: see the bride's answers to these questions on pg. 79!

A Borrowed Item

Good for: _____

Use by: _____

Something Blue

Something Blue represents purity, fidelity, and love. The color is a symbol of the qualities that compose a happy marriage, such as trust, loyalty, and devotion. Blue offers a calming tone and a strong message. It is confident yet cool. It is love. It is the foundation of a good friendship. It is luck. Blue has been a staple wedding color for centuries. It might seem untraditional to choose a blue wedding dress now, but the history of wearing blue actually predates the traditional white wedding gown. Less bold brides looking to incorporate a hint of blue into their look might wear a subtle blue bridal sash or garter belt instead. Whereas blue undies are an unseen and shy idea (except for later), blue shoes can help a bride's personality pop and shine with each step. Something blue isn't pointing to the color's conversational reference about feeling down. Quite the contrary, its colorful placement in the bride's big day evokes loyal feelings relevant to friendship.

Paste in a Keepsake
that Defines your
Relationship with
Your Bridesmaid!

A Colorful Past

White wasn't and still isn't the only standard for a traditional wedding gown. In the Middle Ages, blue was the color of choice for brides because it was a symbol of purity. Blue was a symbolic color for constancy and chastity during biblical times. Today, Japanese brides still wear dresses in various colors. American brides wore red during the Revolutionary War to voice their rebellious beliefs. Some cultures view wearing red as bad luck, but Chinese, Indian, and other Eastern cultures view wearing red as good luck. A bride that wants to wear black might be inspired to make a statement, and she certainly would, since black tends to signify mourning. It is considered unlucky for a bride to wear green because it implies her dress acquired grass stains after she was rolling around on the ground doing something scandalous. (Why she couldn't be given the benefit of the doubt about wanting to roll down the hill for the childhood fun of it is uncertain.) Meanwhile, a bridesmaid not incorporating green into her garb might turn into an old maid!

A COLORFUL BRIDAL PARTY

One of the major decisions a bride makes when planning her wedding is developing a color scheme. Luckily for her (and maybe not you), she will probably look to rely on a colorful cast of bridesmaid characters to help guide her through the psychotic breaks and meltdowns she encounters along the way. Helping the bride's vision bloom from the seeds she has kept locked away in her childhood brain into some beautiful creation is a lot of pressure. Bridesmaids might encounter the brunt of the bride's emotional panic attacks during this planning process, but let these friendships be the glue that ensures the bride will be wearing the right kind of white on her big day. Straightjackets aren't making any appearances on the runway and hopefully won't be down the aisle, either!

CHOOSING BRIDESMAID DRESS COLORS

Imagine a bride's irrational thoughts. She fears the shade of green she chose for the bridesmaids to wear isn't quite as shabby chic in person. What if the five computer monitors she examined the dresses on didn't quite do the seemingly-perfect mint green tone justice? What if, after arriving in the mail, the dress makes every bridesmaid feel a puke green pit growing in her stomach, realizing she's going to have to wear this heinous shade and be photographed in it, smiling? Sage was all the rage, but the designer didn't deliver. What bride could have known that nabbing a stellar deal from another country was going to lead to inaccurate paint swatches and skin tone sagas? Maybe the bride was trying a little too hard to match some vision she saw in a magazine and instead ended up making her bridesmaids look like a bunch of circus clowns! Did you ever imagine how you would react if the bride ever committed such a fashion blunder?

What Kind of Bridesmaid Are You?

Are you the type that would step in to prevent a bad ending from happening, or are you the type to go with the flow, fully prepared to pick up the pieces after they fall? Bridesmaids don't just come in all shapes and sizes, they come from different upbringings with possibly different world views—and a wide range of personality types. So, what kind of bridesmaid are you?

THE KOOKY CONTROL FREAK

Probably a type A troop leader, you thrive on taking control of any and all decisions related to party planning. You scoff at not putting 150 percent effort into everything you do in life. Whether it's completing a crossword puzzle, organizing your closet, or getting a promotion at work, you take it seriously and want to succeed. While this trait can be a great leadership quality that leads to a structured and well-planned calendar of events that glisten and glow, just be conscious that you are one of a group. The bride is likely counting on you to be a leader. Remember that the best leadership is inspired by a humble heart.

THE NICE NEGOTIATOR

A natural-born mediator, you are the one that talks the bride down from a ledge and convinces the other bridesmaids losing their patience to not drop out of the wedding altogether. When there's drama, you are the equalizer. When there's hurt feelings, you are the cheerleader. You deliver comments in a calm tone and listen to others in the spirit of a tree unwavering in the wind. Weddings are stressful, and you are the much-needed glue that holds everyone together. Just be mindful of your own feelings and role in everything. Don't be afraid to stand up for yourself, the bride, or another bridesmaid when drama is brewing.

THE EXCITED PLANNER

You have the best of intentions when sending the bride notes and messages reminding her where and when she should plan things. You are constantly coming up with cute ideas anyway, so this wedding is the perfect opportunity to let your creativity shine! Your assistance and deal-finding skills are a great asset, and the bride will surely appreciate your suggestions to help. Just know that while all of your ideas are obviously fabulous, the bride might have something else in mind. Her artistic choices are not a reflection of your taste. Keep sending those ideas—the bride will love you for it.

THE HOPEFUL CRAFTER

Hello artsy maid! You are the one the bride calls when she has a DIY craft in mind. You like to experiment with paint, glue, markers, and all of the glitter. The bride needs handmade centerpieces? You've got that task down pat. While you are awesome at all of the homemade projects, don't feel like you need to become the bride's elf that crafts all of her requests in some lame North Pole knockoff basement. You are already investing your time and energy, and she will understand if you can't commit to writing the calligraphy for hundreds of wedding invitations. You probably have a job and a life, and she respects that!

THE LAID-BACK UNDERACHIEVER

Let's face it: You are reliable and awesome, but you don't give a damn about weddings. You are here because you love the bride and you value the role she hopes you will play on her big day. Other than that, you go with it, and don't need (or want) to be in charge of any of it. You have a busy life and value your friendship, but you already have enough on your plate without having to worry about this wedding business. You'd really just rather not, but you love the bride, and so you're here. She's happy you are here, too, and that she can rely on you to go with the flow.

THE PARTNER IN CRIME

You are the bridesmaid that wouldn't think twice about buying a plane ticket to another country in the middle of the night if you suspected the bride went off the deep end and was planning on doing something stupid. Partners in crime are the best because they can be a voice of reason when necessary, yet a scheming accomplice when appropriate. Spontaneity and having fun with the bride is what you are all about. Fret not about the lifestyle changes that come with marriage. You and the bride will find new adventures to share together, and something spontaneous is always around the corner.

THE DRAMA QUEEN

Oh, dear, you love drama and probably obsess over reality television reruns! You find your blood pressure boiling when someone says something that doesn't jive with your own feelings. You have great intentions but often a short temper! You love being the center of attention but likewise have the bride's best interests at heart. Someone gets impatient and says something unflattering about the bride? Not on your watch. Someone thinks the bride is being too pushy? You have to talk yourself out of putting this person in a headlock. You're a bodyguard of a best friend, really, but keep in mind the bride probably doesn't want drama behind the scenes.

THE GRADE SCHOOL OLDIE

Even though you now live far away and don't see the bride as often as you would like, you have always considered one another family. On the rare occasions you do see one another, it's as if no time has passed. You are the person that knows the bride best. All of the other girls have probably heard stories about you! You are the bride's roots: a reminder of who she once was and who she wanted to become. You knew her when she was still growing into who she is now. You were at the forefront of her life, and now she is blessed to have you by her side as she moves forward in matrimony.

THE PARTY GIRL

Why live for the weekend? You are a free spirit that craves excitement on every corner, every day of the week. The monotony of the working world has you down and out, and you can't figure out why more people don't look for reasons to party and escape from it. Whether you are single and ready to mingle or you have a significant other that you've happily snatched up, you are the type of person that needs to spend time with her friends. You are the most excited about the chance to celebrate this epic occasion with the bride and her besties, and you'll surely be the life of the party.

THE HOT MAMA

You are a happy, grown-up woman that is completely satisfied with her life and daily routine. You are all about celebrating with the bride, but you are also all about naps and bedtimes. The idea of a late-night bachelorette party is either giving you anxiety or complete excitement. You might dread the break from the daily routine because it throws a wrench into the structure of real life. On the other hand, you might thrive on the idea of an excuse to get out of the house! Whichever type of hot mama you are, just know that the bride is ecstatic you have decided to be here.

ALL SISTERS

Every type of bridesmaid is like family to the bride and groom. You and the bride have your own stories and shared experiences. Maybe you have known her the longest. Maybe you are the most recent addition to the bride's life. It doesn't matter. She values the past, present, and future. Let this time offer nostalgic recollections of childhood that made you want to surround yourself with strong women for the long haul of life. A bridal party should rekindle the happiness found in Girl Scout troops, dance classes, or recreational sports teams. The old song still rings true:

Make new friends,
but keep the old.
One is silver,
the other is gold.

The bride may flaunt her diamond ring. She may prefer silver over gold, or vice versa. But the real gems in her life are the people that support her and enlighten her. Are you the rusty, dependable friend from the past? Are you the shiny new friend from the present? Rather than competing with the other bridesmaids, remember that your personalities and backgrounds are complementary to one another and represent many pieces of the bride's personal story.

A Colorful White Wedding

This is the color that best represents your personality:

_____

_____

_____

_____

_____

This is what your personality brings to my bridal party:

_____

_____

_____

_____

_____

This is the quality you bring out in my personality:

_____

_____

_____

_____

_____

This is the gemstone I imagine you'd be:

_____

_____

_____

_____

_____

This is why your birthstone is perfect:

_____

_____

_____

_____

This is why our friendship is unbreakable:

_____

_____

_____

_____

A Circle of Love

Did you know that the word church derives from circle? It's no great surprise that the circular shape of a ring is a symbol of everlasting love. Like a circle continues on, the couple promises, "till death do us part." The wedding ceremony becomes a human expression of something divine. There will be no end on Earth. Of course, there was a beginning. The history of the engagement ring traces back to Ancient Rome (big surprise). In the 2nd century BC, a woman was often provided with two rings: a gold one for showing off in public, and an iron one for doing work around the house. It really was admirable to be a practical person back then. Some historians also refer to a Roman custom in which wives wore rings attached to small keys, which apparently made reference to being owned by their husbands. Hey, it could have been worse. At least love-struck Roman chicks weren't wearing metal shackles around their wrists. Wonder Woman wasn't created yet, so even optimists wouldn't have been able to make the best of it with a neighborhood game of superhero role playing.

A SYMBOL OF ENGAGEMENT

It wasn't until 1477 when Archduke Maximillian of Austria (talk about a warrior name) decided to offer his betrothed, Mary of Burgundy (also a legit name), a diamond engagement ring, which sparked a frenzy for frosting. Leave it to a little sparkle to make the ladies swoon and forget all about that weird key situation. There was also the fact that Pope Innocent III instituted a mandatory waiting period between betrothal and marriage back in the Middle Ages, and thank goodness he did. Could you imagine if all it took was one question and one yes, and the wedding planning ended at that? Talk about lame! Bridesmaids would be so bored without the drama of the waiting period. Women need drama to survive in the 21st century, otherwise we would all die from boredom. Everyone knows that.

SOMETHING SPARKLY

Romans were romantic even if they tried to play rough around the edges. They thought diamonds were splinters from the falling stars that graced the tips of arrows used by Eros, the god of love. Greeks thought diamonds were teardrops from the gods. The pickup lines dudes used back then were either epic or awful. It's hard to deny the magic that surrounds gazing deep into a diamond, especially when it's shining on the finger that holds the special vein that leads directly to the heart. Romantics lose their breath over it. The ring finger on the left hand is a one-way ticket to the aorta (or something like that), and it's hard to deny such power as a bride-to-be that's deeply in love.

TOUGH AS NAILS

Diamonds are pure carbon and literally the hardest stone out there. Seriously. They are, like, perfectly unbreakable. They're a ten! The unbeatable, unbreakable wrestler of the gemstone bunch! Actually, diamonds really are a ten on this thing called the Mohs scale of mineral hardness. The Mohs scale is simple, really. Stones are measured based on their breakability of other stones. If one gemstone is able to scratch another gemstone, it's considered more durable, thus higher on the scale. It's a good thing gemstones don't have feelings. If gemstones were people, would they be mean girls?

UNBREAKABLE BEST FRIENDS

The idea that diamonds are a girl's best friend is fitting for Hollywood, but what about the real world? A girl's best friend might not be the hardest rock on the block. In fact, best friends are often bendable, flexible, and even soft at heart when it comes to being there for a girl that needs a hug or a heartfelt talk. Friends are hardly made by deciding which person can out-scratch the other. That sounds more like a cat fight than a hen party. Usually the best friendships are built on the idea that one person is capable of letting go when another is holding on, and vice versa. That means blowing with the wind, and knowing when to stand up against it. Diamonds are forever, but if a girl is lucky, so are friends.

Some Kind of Birthright

While bridesmaids may be considered protectors of the bride in human form, bridesmaids themselves might think about seeking their own protection offered as a birthright. Superstition has it that birthstones may be a shield against all kinds of evil and disease. Colors and stones have long held meaning to ancient civilizations looking to gain not only protection, but healing powers and inspiration. Birthstones representative of different months have evolved over time, since ancient folks only differentiated these natural beauties by color. It's similar to how a mechanically-challenged modern woman might tell the difference between two cars. There's the blue one, and the red one.

JANUARY: GARNET

Dark red is the most common shade of garnet. Named after pomegranate, it is believed to help turn thoughts into reality. It doesn't mean wearing garnet is going to turn you into a squirrel if you think long and hard about squirrels. It just means you might garner the confidence to go after that job you've always wanted. A garnet pendant should keep you safe as you travel to the interview.

FEBRUARY: AMETHYST

Amethyst is a royal powerhouse stone that protects the wearer from negative energy and, sadly, wine. Amethyst is associated with the wine god, Bacchus. (Bridesmaid, now you know who to pray to when wedding planning gets overwhelming.) A great healing tool for any insomniacs or grief-stricken saps, wearing amethyst could be a healthy motivator to stop pounding glasses of adult grape juice every night.

MARCH: AQUAMARINE

Aquamarine is believed to provide courage, mental clarity, and good health. It has always had ties to the healing and cleansing nature of the sea, offering a shield against, or even better, providing a surfboard to ride out the waves of life. Aquamarine is considered a tool to center the mind and spirit in the same way a sweet island vacation would during the dead of winter. Maybe a March baby bridesmaid could help the bride and groom plan their honeymoon!

APRIL: DIAMOND

Diamonds have always been an epic representation of true love. First of all, they are known to have supreme healing power as an energy amplifier and a representation of all that is pure in the soul. They are a symbol of accepting spiritual destiny, therefore the perfect pick for expressing true love in a soulmate. It is also said that diamond rings bring courage. Is that why so many lovestruck men are willing to get down on one knee in public?

MAY: EMERALD

May you have strength, the birthstone of May! Emeralds are thought to offer some pretty kooky fore-sight. Word has it that if you place one under your tongue, you'll be able to see the future. Just don't choke on it, because then the future would involve the hospital. Emeralds have ties to the past, too. Cleopatra was a fan, and they have long been associated with love, compassion, and eternal youth. Ancient Romans even dedicated emeralds to Venus, the goddess of love. Maybe that's why people think emeralds can heal heartbreak!

JUNE: PEARL

Pearls are unique gemstones because they are born at sea. Perhaps their ties to the tides of the ocean are what made ancient people think they were magically connected to the moon. Ancient Chinese cultures thought pearls were fit to defend against fire and dragons, ancient Egyptians were buried with them, ancient Greeks thought they were Aphrodite's tears of joy, and ancient Romans believed they belonged to the noble class. Normal peeps could only afford them after the creation of curated pearls in the 1900s, and since then, they have maintained an elegant depiction of pure innocence.

JULY: RUBY

Rubies are the third hardest stone out there. Rubies inspire courage in their wearers, offering ideas of safety and peace on the journey toward accomplishing goals and overcoming fears. Their insides mirror the blood flow that brings life to those wearing the stones. They are representations of pure passion, carrying a life force toward success, wealth, and wisdom.

AUGUST: PERIDOT

Another green gem not to be forgotten is peridot, the gemstone with a more yellowish shade of green that the Egyptians thought protected against nightmares. It's speculated that some of Cleopatra's famous emeralds may have actually been peridots. A positive energy stone, these gems apparently vibrate with the energy of the sun. That's a party trick that protects the wearer from negative emotions of anger, anxiety, and emotional duress.

SEPTEMBER: SAPPHIRE

Sapphires are the third hardest mineral in the world (along with rubies), but their lasting structure is hardly the end of their appeal. While often known for their blue tones, sapphires come in a variety of colors. A symbol of fidelity, wisdom, and clarity, sapphires symbolize the unbreakable structure of a strong relationship. Actually, sapphires were once the preferred stone of engagement rings before diamonds pulled ahead in the early 20th century—not that it's a horse race or anything.

OCTOBER: OPAL

Opal appears in nature in a variety of colors, and glimmers by light passing through tiny spheres of silica within the stone. No two opals are ever the same because of this rainbow magic. Ancient Romans thought opal was a symbol for love and hope and Greeks believed opals gave wearers protection from disease and epic foresight. However, opals gained a bad rap during the 19th and 20th centuries when their popularity threatened diamond traders. It was rumored opal would bring bad luck to wearers not born in October. Diamonds don't need mean girl–smearing to rule the world, but maybe they are more human than they seem.

NOVEMBER: CITRINE & TOPAZ

Citrine is an orange-toned healing quartz that promotes energy in its wearer. The stone is a symbol of happiness and prosperity. It's also associated with money, power, and fortune. The light yellowish color is thought to be a spirit-lifting mood-lightener, providing the much-needed rays of sunshine humans crave in all kinds of weather. Topaz is also a powerful birthstone, but in a way that calms and soothes the wearer. It's connected to creativity, intelligence, and strength—a trifecta of awesome in a person.

DECEMBER: ZIRCON & TURQUOISE

Zircon sounds like a warlord from another planet, but it's actually a very pretty gemstone right here on Earth. It's been said to carry the power to heal pain, protect travelers, and prevent nightmares. Before cold medicine, peeps in the Middle Ages thought this stone could help provide a good night's rest. Not to be outdone is the more vulnerable turquoise. People have long held the belief that blue turquoise has special powers. Native American tribes wore it as a shield of protection. Not only is it a motivator of wisdom and truth, it's a gorgeous accessory against any skin tone or dress color.

QUIZ

Bridesmaid,
How Well Do You Know the Bride?

It's actually not unheard of for a woman in love to be presented with an engagement stone other than a diamond. Victorians were the first to popularize the idea that diamonds could be mixed with other beautiful gemstones to create an epic blend of sparkle on a band. An even bolder route, and no less beautiful, is when someone decides on no diamond altogether! When it's your birthstone you're wearing, its qualities are thought to be amplified. When it's not your birthstone, there's no harm in believing you're still in good hands (except for that one opal rumor). No matter what level of hardness, every stone has unique aspects that make it stand out from the rest. Maybe bridesmaids are the human versions of the stones they wear, except softer, more pliable, and definitely less mean.

Who does the bride admire most? _____

What is the bride's birthstone? _____

Where does the bride want to go on her honeymoon? _____

When did the bride realize the groom was *the one*? _____

Note: see the bride's answers to these questions on pg. 85!

A Colorful Idea

Good for: _____

Use by: _____

And a Silver Sixpence in her Shoe

And a Silver Sixpence in her Shoe is the final piece of a bride's good luck puzzle on her wedding day. In spite of being a lesser-known lucky charm, the sixpence was once counted on to deliver future happiness. The sixpence was first used in the British Empire in 1551 and last circulated a little over four centuries later. The British custom was for the father of the bride to place a sixpence in his daughter's shoe to wish the couple happiness and prosperity in their new marriage. Maybe the hope was for the new couple to step into good fortune? Back then, lucky coins were thought to offer a shield of protection. One Scottish custom even had the groom placing a coin under his foot for good luck. In the late 17th century, the sixpence was often included in the dowry gift to the groom. It then evolved to the bride placing it in her left shoe. Every dad wants his baby girl to hit it rich, and a daughter meeting the right man to spend her life with is worth much more than a few pennies. It is luck. Symbolically, the sixpence is meant to derail the uncertainty of financial gambles and instead facilitate security and wealth.

Paste in a Keepsake
of the Most
Cherished Memory
Shared with Your
Bridesmaid!

A Priceless Offering

You might feel spent by the end of this process, bridesmaid, but you are valued and your contributions are priceless. Bridesmaids offer a reliable reminder of a bride's past, an honest investment in a friendly future, a shared calendar of dates, and a colorful collection of countless memories. As the bride puts one foot in front of the other down the aisle toward the rest of her life, she takes comfort in knowing she has your support.

THE FINAL COUNTDOWN

Dearest bridesmaid, know that there is a light at the end of this tunnel. There is an Emerald City! You will get there. Rest assured, there is an end to this madness of wedding planning. That does not mean there will be an end to your place in the bride's life. This rollercoaster ride is not slowing down yet, not until the beautiful planning comes to fruition and sees its day. You have given the bride the opportunity to trust and believe her wedding day will work out seamlessly. You're a gem of a bodyguard, bridesmaid, built in the exact perfect shape you should be, looking fab in whatever garb you are wearing, smiling your true spirit. You seriously rock.

THE REHEARSAL DINNER

Like any great show, a wedding requires a lot of planning and at least one rehearsal. After all of the contemplating over different choices and decisions about what to eat and when to say cheese, it's time to celebrate and casually finalize the details. Typically, the bridal party will be invited to meet with the bride and groom the night before the wedding at the ceremony site to run through exactly what everyone will be doing on the big day. Bridesmaids will learn where to stand, how to walk, and when to give the bride a wink and cheers of bubbly. All of that standing around can leave people hungry. Luckily there is usually a dinner that the bridal party and out-of-town guests can enjoy. Traditionally, the groom's family will host. However, every family is different and the host may depend on what makes sense for each couple. All that bridesmaids have to know is that they don't need to worry about hosting this event. They just need to show up! This is usually when the bride will offer her wedding gift to you for being so utterly fabulous.

THE FINAL TOUCHES

Bridesmaid bodyguards helped the bride make it this far—now they have reached the last stretch of hill before the promised land. A bridesmaid's role on the morning and day of the wedding is still ever-important. The maid of honor holds a particularly significant spot in making sure the day runs smoothly. Unless there is something prohibiting a bridesmaid from arriving early, she should be present when the bride is getting ready, whether the site of preparation is on the ceremony grounds or at the bride's home. Bridesmaids should quadruple check that they have everything they need for the night. The dress. The shoes. The jewelry. Typically, the bridal party accompanies the bride to the ceremony site. Sometimes, they like to enjoy some bubbly along the way. Keep it classy, though. Remember the superstition about bridesmaids stumbling down the aisle!

HAIR & MAKEUP

It's been said that a bride should have only a happily married woman do her hair for the wedding. Just as a bride's wedding day makeup should complement her everyday beauty, a bridesmaid should not feel pressured to put on more makeup than normal. Of course, it's okay to step up your game and go a little glam. Whatever you do should blend with the other women in the bridal party. Just don't feel like you need to play dress-up as someone else. It's nice to get your hair and makeup done for a wedding, but it can be expensive. Bridesmaids should be offered a choice to do their own hair and makeup or have it done for them. If the bride really wants you to get yours done, don't be shy about telling her it's not really in your budget. An understanding bride may opt to make the payment for you rather than forcing you to pay for something that really is just an added expense on her itinerary.

THE CEREMONY

The maid of honor will be in charge of making sure everyone knows their place. This is where the rehearsal aspect of the night comes into play. Everyone will be excited and eager for the ceremony to start. Try not to sweat the small stuff. Remember the bride and her family are probably pretty anxious, feeling a flood of emotions as they wait to experience this incredible moment in front of so many loved ones. It's easy to get caught up in the chaos. Try to keep everyone calm. Help solidify the bride's look by making sure her veil and dress are perfect. No bride wants to walk down the aisle with a piece of her gown stuck in her underwear. As you look her over, remind her to add a tiny item to her ensemble to make sure her soul isn't lost in any mirrors! As the ceremony progresses, try to take it all in and feel the love. This is a very special moment, a much-awaited, long-anticipated moment. You don't want to miss it. Once the marriage is sealed with a kiss, it's time to celebrate! Strut your stuff back down the aisle and give the bride a big hug and a high five. Tell her to put on her dancing shoes. If the reception is at a different location, help the group get together to travel there. If the reception is at the same venue, jump up and down and get ready to party.

THE WEDDING RECEPTION

This is it, bridesmaid! This is the fun part. This is where all of your senses can appreciate all of the planning. See the beauty. Smell the flowers. Taste the food. Hear the music. Feel the love. The only thing left for you to do is help the bride celebrate. Remember, she enlisted you to help her enjoy every aspect of this day. That's based on your history. That's based on who you are as a person. Whether you are superstitious or not, the bride is counting on you to send good vibes. Now is the time to whip out your superhero friendship qualities! That's easy, because all you have to do is enjoy the day and be the incredible friend you have always been. Don't forget to meet and greet the wedding guests throughout the night. Introduce yourself to the family members you haven't met before. Defuse any drama. Light up the dance floor. Spread the love and share in the magic of the cherished moments. Remind the bride to eat and remind the couple to take a few moments to enjoy one another. If you are the maid of honor, don't worry too much about your speech. Speak from the heart. If you aren't the maid of honor, provide a pep talk and give the girl a boost of confidence. Make sure you laugh at her jokes and tell her to keep them in good taste!

THE AFTER-PARTY

The after-party isn't just about keeping the party going once the music has softened and the grandparents have become sleepy. It's not just about finding the bar that's still open. It's not only about extending this wonderful day a few hours longer. It's about what comes after. It's the married life. As everyone sends their well-wishes to the bride and groom, take comfort in knowing your bonds with the bride will only continue to grow after this. The bride and groom have agreed to grow old together. That commitment is an unspoken vow you share with the bride as friends for life.

Now, Paste in
Those Wedding
(And After-Party)
Photos!

Now, Paste in
Those Wedding
(And After-Party)
Photos!

Now, Paste in
Those Wedding
(And After-Party)
Photos!

Now, Paste in
Those Wedding
(And After-Party)
Photos!

Now, Paste in
Those Wedding
(And After-Party)
Photos!

Now, Paste in
Those Wedding
(And After-Party)
Photos!

Now, Paste in
Those Wedding
(And After-Party)
Photos!

A Final Thank You

I know I can count on you because . . .

_____

_____

_____

_____

_____

_____

_____

I am most excited about . . .

_____

_____

_____

_____

_____

_____

_____

I hope we don't forget . . .

_____

_____

_____

_____

_____

_____

_____

This is a time we laughed:

_____

_____

_____

_____

_____

_____

_____

This is a time we cried:

_____

_____

_____

_____

_____

_____

_____

This is another experience I look forward to sharing with you:

_____

_____

_____

_____

_____

_____

_____

A Toast to Friendship

The bride will soon be singing your praises, bridesmaid, as she has always has done. Whether it's slurred karaoke platonic love professions or downright genuine girl talk, this message is about expressing deep appreciation and respect. Thank you, bridesmaid. Simply, you are the best representation of friendship, sisterhood, and love. Completely, you are unique, vibrant, and irreplaceable. You are adored and saluted for all you have done to earn this role. You are awesome.

A LASTING PROMISE

Family and friends gather to honor a happy couple's love and devotion, but a lucky girl has many loves in her life. One is the romantic love to last a lifetime. That's the groom that makes her heart flutter. Beyond that romance, there are other loves that support a bride's heart when she's struggling. There are other loves that lift her spirits higher when she's already happy. The blood of family. The beauty of friendship. That's you, bridesmaid. You have always been factored into this equation of lasting love. Except, as women age and other responsibilities arise, it becomes increasingly difficult to maintain friendships shared over bowls of ice cream and bottles of wine. Friendships have to adapt to survive the evolution into adulthood and motherhood. Adulthood is a loose term, because really, what fun girl ever wants to grow up anyway? It's really a suggestion more than anything. Still, accepting new responsibilities as an old lady does not mean a sisterhood loses its value as time goes on. It's easy to lose touch and become busy as daily life routines and adult commitments get in the way, but it's important that women stay deeply connected with the friends and sisters that know them best. Love and marriage are a new chapter ahead, but the roots that have kept this bride so grounded and supported are what will continue to enhance her life, her future, and her hope for your place in it.

A HEARTFELT KEEPSAKE

Women are strong. Brides are stronger. Bridesmaids are the strength in the background. Chicks can craft their own glory boxes. Women can propose to men. Girls can party. Girls can rock. Girls can play! Every tradition has a beginning, but every day is a new beginning and an invitation to impact the future. Modern bridal parties have the power to make their own history and rewrite the book on how to do weddings their own way. This collection of anecdotes, traditions, and heartfelt offerings is meant to serve as a giant, gracious thank you, dearest bridesmaid. You have given the bride a precious gift just by being who you are. You define nobility and utter awesomeness. Nothing could possibly capture what your friendship truly means to the bride, but she hopes this heartfelt keepsake comes close. Thank you, dearest bridesmaid, for showering the bride with love, celebrating her singlehood with spirit, and cherishing a ceremony she is so happy you have agreed to be a part of. The bride in your life hopes this text will forever be inked as a promise to stay in one another's lives. Beyond change, beyond time, beyond distance—you belong in the bride's heart, and it is there you will stay long after she marries her soul mate. Thank you, dearest bridesmaid, for all of the old stories, the new experiences, the borrowed clothes, the colorful memories, and the priceless friendship.

QUIZ

*Bridesmaid,
How Well Do You Know the Bride?*

Who did the bride call first when she got engaged? _____

What would the bride do with a million dollars? _____

Where does the bride want to settle down? _____

When did the bride get her first job? _____

Note: see the bride's answers to these questions on pg. 85!

A Priceless Adventure

Good for: _____

Use by: _____

Bride's Answer Key

SOMETHING OLD QUIZ ANSWERS

Who did the bride want to marry when she was a little girl? _____

What was the bride's favorite childhood hobby? _____

Where was the bride born? _____

When did the bride realize you were awesome? _____

SOMETHING NEW QUIZ ANSWERS

Who would play the bride in a movie? _____

What is the bride's favorite hobby as an adult? _____

Where did the bride meet the groom? _____

When did the bride say YES to the groom? _____

SOMETHING BORROWED QUIZ ANSWERS

Whose wardrobe does the bride want to raid? _____

What material item can the bride not live without? _____

Where does the bride love to shop? _____

When did/will she know the dress is *the one*? _____

SOMETHING BLUE QUIZ ANSWERS

Who does the bride admire most? _____

What is the bride's birthstone? _____

Where does the bride want to go on her honeymoon? _____

When did the bride realize the groom was *the one*? _____

AND A SILVER SIXPENCE IN HER SHOE QUIZ ANSWERS

Who did the bride call first when she got engaged? _____

What would the bride do with a million dollars? _____

Where does the bride want to settle down? _____

When did the bride get her first job? _____

Acknowledgments

- This heartfelt keepsake would not have been possible without the relationships I built over time and the support and inspiration I received from family and loved ones. My father Michael's wit, coaching, and creative accomplishments led me to follow in his footsteps as a writer. My mother Judy's guidance, strength, and thoughtful compassion inspired me to lead a balanced life. I am thankful for the confidence and sense of humor instilled by my parents and brothers. Morgan's lasting impact on others showed me the importance of being a true friend. Matt's relentless drive and knack for storytelling inspired me to share meaningful stories of my own. Martin's fearless resilience and passion for photography helped me see life in treasured moments.

- I didn't grow up with sisters, but I am thankful to have found some along the way. Without these women, I would not have experienced being a bridesmaid or had any reason to understand the value of that role today. My dearest Michelle, Jenny A., Anastasia, Jackie, Jenny L., P-Dawg, Christy, and Jeanette are the inspiration for this project. Our shared memories, lasting friendships, and funny inside jokes are what planted the seeds for this idea.

- I must also thank my flower girls, Skyeler and Hannah, for making me think about the future of bridesmaids, and my nephews, Loukas and Ethan, for keeping our wedding rings safe.

- Thank you, Karen at Isabelle's, for making me feel like a princess in your bridal shop.

- Thank you, Gary Flom Photography, for capturing our special day so perfectly.

- I am grateful for the Olde Mill Inn, which provided a beautiful setting for Nick and I to celebrate our love.

- Thank you, Mr. & Mrs. Thomas LaPlaca, for raising Nick to be the kind of gentleman I always dreamed of marrying.

- Thank you, Nick, for being a caring, funny, and understanding man that fully supported my journey writing this as we planned our own wedding. True love is finding patience when a deep-thinking bride obsesses over bridesmaid dress colors and other wedding details.

- Finally, I must thank Nicole Mele and Skyhorse Publishing for sharing a creative vision for what this book could become while making it all possible. I am most grateful.